Lotta Suter

# YONA

# SARAI

# RUWTH

## The Complete Libretti
## to a Chamber Opera Trilogy
## by Robert W. Griffin

Beinn Ard Publishing
Hollis, NH 03409
www.beinnard.com

For more information on these chamber operas, including on obtaining the scores , see www.beinnard.com.

ISBN: 978-1-889314-28-0 (hardcover)
ISBN: 978-1-889314-29-7 (paperback)
ISBN: 978-1-889314-30-3 (eBook)
ISBN: 978-1-889314-31-0 (ePDF)

Library of Congress Control Number: 2014935426

First edition April 2014

Printed in the United States of America

*To all our friends*
*who joined us in creating these chamber operas*

# Contents

# RUWTH: a chamber opera

# Imagining Yona, Sarai, and Ruwth

The libretti to this trilogy of chamber operas tell the stories of the well-known biblical figures of Jonah, Sarah and Ruth in a new light – therefore the phonetic transliteration of their Hebrew names into Yona and Ruwth, or in the case of Sarai the use of her original name. This kind of re-imagining of the ancient tales is most alive in the Jewish Midrash tradition. That is where I found many valuable sources for my own writing. Wikipedia defines Midrash as "a method of interpreting biblical stories that goes beyond simple distillation of religious, legal, or moral teachings. It fills in gaps left in the biblical narrative regarding events and personalities that are only hinted at."

What interested me most in all three stories were questions of justice. It started with my re-acquaintance with Yona, such a stubborn man – and yet a person with integrity. His strong sense of justice did not bow to power, but neither was it softened by mercy.

This ambivalence of justice, its vertical and horizontal dimension so to speak, is also the main theme of <u>Sarai</u>. Here we experience the conflict in the realm of religion. On one side we see Abraham cherishing his "sacred secret covenant" with God, a man who is willing to sacrifice human life for a higher justice. On the other side we find Sarai and Hagar, the mothers of Abraham's children Ishmael and Isaac, who say: "We worship heaven in the birth of our children, in a moment of laughter and in the hours of grief".

In the story of <u>Ruwth</u> the struggle for justice is taken from heavenly spheres down to earth. The community of Bethlehem has to decide how to receive the impoverished widow Na'omi and her Moabite daughter-in-law. It is not easy for the villagers to accept the newcomers and share food and shelter with the two women. חסד (chesed), the loving-kindness of Ruwth and Boaz foremost, helps their people to transcend long-established communal customs and create a more universal and inclusive society.

Each libretto in this book is preceded by a short introduction which contains more information concerning the background of these works. These outlines also examine the music to which the texts are set by the composer Robert W. Griffin. For example: How are certain characters or choruses represented in the orchestration? Which musical traditions do echo in this music? Readers interested to learn more about the musical side of <u>Yona</u>, <u>Sarai</u> and <u>Ruwth</u> might want to have a look at the score (i.e. on www.beinnard.com).

YONA

YONA

# Introduction

*Yona* is the contemporary phonetic rendering of the Hebrew name יוֹנָה, Jonas, which means "Dove".

Children of many generations have been greatly impressed by the story of Yona in the belly of the whale and imagined the deep darkness of the "big fish" and the miraculous landing on safe shore. But the Book of Yona also contains a different story. The Christian, the Judaic and the Islamic narrative all show this prophet must have been a rather stubborn man: He knew how to tell right from wrong and he was ready to bet not only his own life but the life and welfare of others on this truth.

This chamber opera explores what such a strong sense of justice could have meant to his own family and the neighbors in his small village. How did it affect his traveling companions on the boat when he ran away from God's command and headed for Tarshish, the farthest place he could imagine? And what did the people of Jerusalem, whom he warned first as a messenger of God, make of Yona? How did the people of Nineveh, who were rescued from destruction by his prophesies, see this man?

While all of the people above are mentioned in the traditional legends, they appear in <u>Yona</u> as individual characters. The story is narrated from the perspective of Yona's fictitious daughter Shachar (the name meaning: morning, dawn). The scenes of the opera are all set in Yona's house. The time is right after the funeral of the prophet, while his daughter is sitting the seven days of Shiva for her father.

<u>Yona</u> is organized according to these seven days of Shiva, the ritual period of mourning in Judaism, during which neighbors and friends of the bereaved family visit the mourners in their house. Traditionally, no greetings are exchanged and visitors wait for the mourners to initiate conversation. Once engaged in conversation by the mourners, it is appropriate for visitors to

talk about the deceased, sharing stories of his or her life. As a farewell, the visitors will often recite these traditional words of consolation: "May the Omnipresent comfort you among all mourners of Zion and Jerusalem. And may you know no more sorrow".

The first day of Shiva, the day of burial, is represented in Yona by the prelude. On the second day, Shachar, the daughter of Yona and his only remaining relative, is alone in her house, she is bitterly angry with her father even in his death. Over the next several days, Shachar is visited by four groups or individuals who reflect on major events in Yona's life: his life in the village; his being cast overboard and swallowed by a whale; his dark prophesying to Jerusalem; and his warning to Nineveh. During the course of these visits, Shachar comes to see her father in a new way and recognizes the difficult calling he took on in his life. At the end of the seventh day she, too, is able to wish that her father may rest in peace.

The music in Yona mirrors the libretto in a number of ways. The harmonic complexity and dissonance increase throughout the first half of the chamber opera, reflecting the complexity that is being revealed about Yona and about Shachar's feelings towards him. This harmonic progression is first hinted at in the prelude, in which the initial D-minor immediately develops into a clashing D and E-flat dissonance in the timpani. The prelude moves through increasingly remote keys, from F-minor to B-flat-minor. The opera as a whole follows a similar progression as it moves to increasingly complex harmonies, climaxing at the center of the opera in Yona's aria.

In this central aria, "In my distress", the most complex of the opera, Yona himself steps forward to speak of his life, as though drawn back into the world by the strong memories of him that are being presented. His dramatic rescue from the depths of the sea becomes the turning point of the music, which returns from the depths of harmonic complexity to brighter major keys in the "Benedicite" songs of blessing, and in the valedictions sung by

Shachar's visitors, ending in the transparent harmonies in Shachar's final solo. Her last word, "peace", which is sung without accompaniment, transforms the harmony of the opera from D-minor to D-major. But the work nonetheless ends in D-minor, so that the orchestral conclusion reflects the continuing ambivalence of Shachar's feelings about her father.

The harmonic complexity is also expressed in the meters used in the chamber opera, with Yona's solo once again the most complex meter of the work. His melody, in 5/4 time, is set against alternating 3/2 and 2/3 divisions of the measure in the orchestration. Shachar's central solo is also in 5/4, but in her case the meter combines the 3/4 and common meter of her visitors, reflecting their influence on her and her feelings at this central point of the chamber opera.

The different worlds of the visitors appear in the orchestration that accompanies them, particularly heard in the woodwinds that accompany the village women and the brass that go with the mariners. Yona, Shachar and the midwife of Jerusalem are closely associated with strings, as is the "great fish", which is given voice by the contrabass. Although the whale is only hinted at in the whale song motif played by the contrabass, the animal too becomes a presence in the chamber opera, an image both of the dark that swallows Yona in his stubbornness and also of the saving grace that brings him back to land and life.

The text of Yona reflects many sources and traditions, including the Bible, the Koran and Moby Dick. The libretto is enriched by these references, such as in the poetic words of the "Benedicite" chorales that are taken from medieval plainsong. In the same way, the music is also enriched by echoes of other works and musical styles, including Jewish folk traditions and Gregorian chant. The triplet motif with which the opera ends is the most direct quotation of any other work. It recalls a similar motif in the final movement of the German Requiem of Johannes Brahms.

There, the single rising triplet on "sterben" (to die) is transformed into a repeated setting for "selig" (blessed) as the chorus proclaims "Blessed are the dead". As in Brahms' piece, in Yona, too, the transformation of this triplet motif from D-minor in the prelude to D-major in the postlude represents in miniature what the music as a whole conveys: the blessing that Shachar is finally able to express for her father.

# Cast of Characters

Shachar, daughter of Yona

Yona, a prophet of Israel

Three women from Shachar's village

Captain and two mariners from Tarshish

Midwife from Jerusalem

Child, woman and man from Nineveh

YONA

# YONA

## 1ˢᵗ DAY OF SHIVA

*The biblical story in this chamber opera about the minor prophet* Yona
*is narrated from the perspective of Yona's daughter* Shachar *(morning,
dawn). The seven scenes of the opera are all set in Yona's house. The
time is right after the funeral of the prophet, while his only daughter is
sitting the seven days of Shiva for her father.*

*This first scene is an instrumental prelude, during which Shachar is
sitting on a low stool in the main room of her father's house. As a ritual
sign of mourning she wears a torn blouse.*

## 2ⁿᵈ DAY OF SHIVA

*This scene opens with Shachar still sitting on her low stool.*

> *Shachar:*
> My blouse is torn across the heart,
> And I have lit the candles
> For seven days of Shiva.
> I mourn my father,
> Yona, son of Amittai,
> A name laden with truth.
>
> Yona's truth knew neither lenity nor warmth.
> It did not make allowances to human weakness.
> Each crime deserved a punishment,
> Each breach of rule called for a fine.
>
> One day, my brother Meir was herding livestock
> Out on the pasture with some other shepherd boys.
> They talked and laughed and played as children do,
> Lost track of time - and lost a couple of their sheep.

Our father could not take this disregard for duty,
He sent the culprit out, alone, to make amends.
He ordered Meir into the stormy night.
The boy obeyed and was thus swallowed by the dark.

My brother Meir did not return, was never seen again.
Our mother blamed her husband for her eldest's fate.
Their marriage grew an open wound that never healed.
We all lived in a house of grief and ire.

If Yona himself suffered too, he never said so.
He went about his daily tasks unfazed, unblinking.
One-hundred-twenty years he lived for truth and justice
And died, adamant, as a righteous man.

'Twas nothing then but truth?

# 3rd DAY OF SHIVA

*Three women from the village enter. They wait for Shachar to speak.*

*Shachar:*
Yona has known you well,
Women from the village.

*First woman from the village:*
We've come to pay respect, daughter of Yona.
Your father took good care of our laws
Within the village. Year after year
He acted as a fair and even judge.

*Second woman from the village:*
When a greedy farmer took water from our fields
To irrigate his own crops in the drought
And our harvest withered, Yona took the thief to task
And had him recompense us for our loss.

*Third woman from the village:*
My husband was a violent man, hitting fast and hard.
Tradition wanted me, the wife, to suffer and accept
The blows and verbal slander. Not Yona, though.
He sent the man away and gave me back my self.

*First and second woman from the village:*
Your father was a stubborn man, we know.
Each part of him was straight, and strict and stern.
Yet he was there and he was just
When justice was most needed.

*All three women from the village:*
Yona's calling was a work of God,
Was blessed and did bless us in return.
We've come to pay respect and praise
A life well lived right to the end.

*The three village women stay in the back of the room. Throughout the entire Shiva period they lead the other visitors in and offer them something to drink and to eat. They are there because according to Jewish tradition mourners should not be left alone. In* Yona *they will also join the different parties in songs of praise.*

## 4th DAY OF SHIVA

*Enter three seamen from the fateful ship Yona boarded a long time ago. They wait for Shachar to speak.*

*Shachar:*
Yona has spoken of you well,
Seamen from Tarshish.

*The sailors start to talk about Yona's journey on their fateful trip to Tarshish. The first sailor steps forward.*

*First sailor:*
Yona was late to come aboard
And then most keen to sail.
A fugitive we thought, an evil-doer.
We didn't want to take him in.
Bad luck such haunted people are,
A curse for ship and men.
But Yona paid his fare up front
And a good prize at that.
He got his stateroom and his berth,
Brought his bags and went to rest
While seamen cast off cables
And from deserted wharf
The ship of Tarshish glided.
The waters though rebelled.
They would not bear
The wicked burden.


*Captain of the ship:*
A mighty storm came on,
The ship was like to break.
Winds were shrieking,
Waves were rolling.
Yet from high above
A white moon shone
On deep black sea.

In great distress we cried to our gods,
Disburdened us and our ship from worldly goods.
One man alone was absent from this fight for life:
Yona was fast asleep, unconscious in the face of danger.
I called to him "What do you mean, you sleeper!
Arise and pray! Maybe *your* God
Will give a thought to us and save us from our sinking."
The mighty storm raged on.

My men were want to cast the lot
So they would know who caused
This uproar of the Heavens.
The lot fell upon Yona.
"Who are you?" they did ask him,
"What is it you have you done?"

Yona replied: "Hebrew I am, and I do fear my Lord,
The God of heaven, who made sea and dry land."
We were exceedingly afraid
To hear this man's confession
In that we knew too well our own shortcomings.
It was with *our* aid and our abetment
That Yona shunned the presence of his God.

*Second sailor:*
The storm grew fiercer still,
The winds were deadly strong.
 "What shall we do?" we asked,
"How can we quiet down the sea?"
Yona said to take him up
And throw him overboard;
The tempest was upon us for his sake.
We didn't want to do that,
Instead worked hard to get to shore.
To no avail, the waters were against us.
Three times we lowered Yona down -
The ocean calmed at once.
But every time we got him back on board
It started up its howling and its screaming.
There was no other way:
We had to give up Yona to God's wrath and fury.

*Captain of the ship:*
We took up Yona and cast him forth into the sea
And the sea ceased from her rage.

*Shachar:*
And God called upon a great fish to swallow up Yona.
And Yona was in the belly of the fish
For three days and three nights.


*The two sailors and the captain step back and form a chorus with the three women from the village. Yona's daughter stands alone in the middle of the room as she thinks about her father's stay in the belly of the big fish.*

*Shachar:*
Swallowed by the dark like Meir –
What is that blackness, Father?
Is it all?  Or is it none?
Does it gently dim the senses?
Or does it wake extreme despair?
Were you afraid there
In the belly of the whale?
Did you repent?
Cry for help?
Or accept your ill-fate too
As justice?

*Yona enters and narrates his ordeal.*

*Yona:*
In my distress I called to the Lord,
And He answered me.
Out of the belly of Sheol I cried,
And He heard my voice.

You cast me into the heart of the seas,
And the flood was round about me;
Waves and billows swept over me.
I thought I had been banished
From Your sight;

Would I ever look again
Upon your holy temple?
The waters reached up to my soul,
The deep closed me in;
Seaweed was wrapped around my head.
I sank to the roots of the mountains.
I went down to the land which barred me in forever.

But you brought my life up from the pit,
O Lord my God.
When my soul fainted within me
I remembered you, Lord,
And my prayer rose to you,
and to your holy temple.
Those who cling to vain idols
forsake their true loyalty.
But I, with a song of thanksgiving,
Will sacrifice to you.
What I have vowed, that I will pay.
Deliverance belongs to the Lord.

*Shachar stands up and steps next to her father, but is unaware of his presence.*

*Shachar:*
And the Lord commanded the fish,
And the fish spit Yona onto dry land.

*Exit Yona. The three village women join the sailors in a song of praise.*

*Chorus of mariners:*
O you Heavens, bless the Lord
O you Waters above the Firmament, bless the Lord
O you Sun and Moon, bless the Lord
O you Stars of Heaven, bless the Lord
O you Showers and Dew, bless the Lord
O you Winds of God, bless the Lord.

*Chorus of village women:*
O you Fire and Heat, bless the Lord
O you Winter and Summer, bless the Lord
O you Frost and Cold, bless the Lord
O you Ice and Snow, bless the Lord
O you Nights and Days, bless the Lord
O you Light and Darkness, bless the Lord.

*Combined chorus of mariners and village women:*
O you Lightnings and Clouds, bless the Lord
O you Wells, bless the Lord
O you Seas and Floods, bless the Lord
O you Whales and all that move in the waters,
bless the Lord
O you Children of Men, bless the Lord
Praise Him and magnify Him forever.

*First sailor and second sailor:*
May the Omnipresent comfort you, daughter of Yona,
Among all mourners of Jerusalem and Zion.

*Captain of the ship:*
And may you know
No more sorrow.

*Exeunt three seamen.*

# 5th DAY OF SHIVA

*Shachar gets up to receive an old woman, a midwife from Jerusalem.*

*Shachar:*
Yona praised you well,
Midwife of Jerusalem.

*The midwife takes Shachar's hand while she starts singing.*

*Midwife:*
I'm well aware, my child, that Yona's life – and yours –
Have never been that easy.
His calling was much heavier than mine,
Placed hardship on himself, his sons and daughters.
I'm midwife mere to virgin babies,
to children without sin,
He however eased the birth of virtue in great sinners.

Many years ago, Yona foretold the downfall of our city.
We in Jerusalem repented and were saved
By God's great mercy.
Your father though was bitter
By reason that his prophesy was not fulfilled
And he himself no longer a famed prophet
But mocked by many and his reputation stained.

Yona no longer wanted to be messenger of God
And only through divine ordeals
He came to terms with his own destiny and fate.
Sadly, he never did embrace himself
The paradox of grace:
That a true prophet sometimes must proclaim
Great doom and damage lest
Doom and damage in earnest be dispensed.

Yona saved Jerusalem
For this we shall say thanks.

O let Israel bless the Lord
O you Priests of the Lord, bless the Lord
O you Servants of the Lord, bless the Lord
O you Spirits and Souls of the Righteous, bless the Lord
O you holy and humble Men of Heart, bless the Lord
Praise Him and magnify Him forever.

*Midwife and Shachar:*
O let Israel bless the Lord
O you Priests of the Lord, bless the Lord
O you Servants of the Lord, bless the Lord
O you Spirits and Souls of the Righteous, bless the Lord
O you holy and humble Men of Heart, bless the Lord
Praise Him and magnify Him forever.

*Midwife:*
May the Omnipresent comfort you, my daughter,
Among all mourners of Jerusalem and Zion.
And may you know
No more sorrow.

*Exit Midwife of Jerusalem.*

# 6th DAY OF SHIVA

*Enter a woman, a man, and a child from Nineveh.*

*Shachar:*
Yona journeyed far to meet you,
People of Nineveh.

*Man from Nineveh:*
Yona saved us from great ill,
Our city was awash in pride and selfishness.
With Yona's help we turned away
From might and gold and strife,
To live life at its fullest.

*Woman from Nineveh:*
Your father did prevent not only bricks and walls
Of Nineveh from certain demolition.
Our heart and minds were vulnerable too,
Jeopardized by callousness and greed
Till Yona's cry brought back compassion.

*Child from Nineveh:*
You must be sad, Shachar, of Yona's death.
I am sad too, as are my brothers.
I brought you something though, some seeds
We kept of the mysterious plant
God gave Yona for comfort.

*Man, woman, and child from Nineveh:*
O let the Earth bless the Lord
O you Mountains and Hills, bless the Lord
O all you Green Things upon the earth, bless the Lord
O you Fowls of the Earth, bless the Lord
O all you Beasts and Cattle, bless the Lord
O you Children of Men, bless the Lord
Praise Him and magnify Him forever.

*People from Nineveh, village women and Shachar:*
O let the Earth bless the Lord
O you Mountains and Hills, bless the Lord
O all you Green Things upon the earth, bless the Lord
O you Fowls of the Earth, bless the Lord
O all you Beasts and Cattle, bless the Lord
O you Children of Men, bless the Lord
Praise Him and magnify Him forever.

*Man and woman from Nineveh:*
May the Omnipresent comfort you, daughter of Yona,
Among all mourners of Jerusalem and Zion.

*Child from Nineveh:*
And may you know
No more sorrow

*Exeunt people from Nineveh.*

*First woman from the village:*
May the Omnipresent comfort you, Shachar,

*Second woman from the village:*
Among all mourners of Jerusalem and Zion.

*Third woman from the village:*
And may you know
No more sorrow.

*Exeunt three women from the village.*

# 7ᵗʰ DAY OF SHIVA

*Shachar stands alone in the room.*

*Shachar:*
Father, you were a driven man,
Laden with truth and justice.
You chose right over love,
Appraised yourself and others.

God's mercy did not soften
Your decree, nor change you, Yona.
Yet as a prophet and a judge
You changed the lives of others.

With that feat I'll learn to be content.
I'll sow the seeds from Nineveh,
To honor you. May you find comfort
In the plant's gentle shade.

*Shachar picks up her little stool, then gives a last blessing.*

*Shachar:*
Yona, son of Amittai,
May he now find peace.

*Shachar removes her torn blouse and leaves the room.*

# SARAI

SARAI

# Introduction

The story of Sarah, Abraham and Isaac is told from the point of view of Sarah, who is called in this work by her original name Sarai. There are countless versions of the legend, also countless - and contradicting – chronologies, especially of Sarai's life. This is one more tentative telling of the ancient tale.

The story is set in six scenes (plus prologue and epilogue) for the six wailings and cries that Sarai let out when she heard of Isaac's binding (sacrifice). Each cry contains a part of her biography in a loosely chronological order. Yet it is the emotional importance that drives the narrative more than historical facts or a biblical literal meaning.

The sound of the shofar (ram's horn) is central to the story of Sarai. To this day on Rosh Hashanah the instruction is to take up the shofar (representing the taking of Isaac to Mount Moriah for sacrifice) and to blow the shofar (representing Sarai's pain and sadness when she hears of Isaac's binding). To this day during the traditional Jewish holiday four different sounds of the shofar are used:

> TEKIAH, a call for the individual to transcend to community, to gather for celebration – or for confrontation. To join forces for a challenge or join hands in gratitude or joy. It is a low blasting sound.

> SHEVARIM, a wailing, mournful sound, hearing the brokenness of the world, a discord in need of resolution, a cry for healing and justice. It is a wailing undulating treble sound.

> TERUAH, a wake-up call, an alarming sound, an urge to move forward towards meaning and knowledge. A treble sound, staccato-like.

TEKIAH GEDOLAH, a sound of hope in the ultimate triumph of goodness and joy. Related to the simple TEKIAH but three times as long.

(Examples of the different shofar sounds can be heard on Youtube. The interpretation above is taken from various sources, but primarily from Rabbi Donald Rossoff, Temple B'nai Or in Morristown, NJ.)

These sounds are an organizing principle of this chamber opera. The shofar serves as the primary indication of the larger musical structure by introducing each of the six scenes with its echo of one of the six cries of Sarai. It also concludes the six scenes by re-stating the TEKIAH GEDOLAH in the final measure of scene six. These scenes are framed by the prologue and epilogue, each of which is introduced by an echo of the shofar's TEKIAH GEDOLAH in the opening chords of the solo violin. The shofar also plays a structural role within the scenes, introducing some changes of location or characters. In addition, the four sounds of the shofar are used as motivic elements in the development of the music, such as in terms of the rhythmic intensity of the TERUAH emerging as a driving force during the sixth scene, particularly in the instrumental depiction of the sacrifice of Isaac.

The characteristic G to D interval of the shofar's TEKIAH, SHEVARIM and TEKIAH GEDOLAH is reflected in the harmonic structure of Sarai. The first four chords of the work alternate   between F minor and B minor, a diminished fifth that resembles but transforms the perfect fifths of the shofar sounds. The six scenes alternate between these two keys; the scenes of conflict (2, 4, 6) are in F minor and the scenes of reconciliation (1, 3, 5) in B minor and the closely associated keys of D major and G major. The alternation of keys also plays a motivic role, reflecting the conflicting worlds confronting Sarai: the destructive world of Abram's obsession and the supportive world of love and friendship. The increasing opposition between these two worlds comes to a head in the sacrifice of Isaac and Sarai's six cries following Isaac's re-telling of that experience. In those six cries of the mother, the opposing chords sound at the same time, in the moment when those worlds come into unbearable conflict for Sarai.

The conflict between those two worlds is also expressed in the rhythm and timbre of the music in the six scenes. As the opera progresses, Abram's world becomes increasingly dark and oppressive, as is reflected in the spare, stark voicing of the instruments that accompany his solos. His world also becomes increasingly conflicted, reflected in the increasing rhythmic uncertainty in his solos and in those of Sarai and Hagar as they speak of or become entangled in his obsession. The shifts of meter in Abram's, Sarai's and Hagar's solos create a world which is unstable, foreign and filled with turmoil. This comes to a head in the music of Isaac's sacrifice, in which the interjected exclamations of the B minor and F minor chords disrupt the already jagged and urgent rhythmic complexity of the music.

The thematic elements of the music contribute to both structure and characterization in Sarai. In the first scene, Sarai's opening solo "When I opened my eyes" introduces a theme that is used for expressions of love throughout the opera; beneath that theme, the strings introduce the theme that is used for expressions of friendship, such as Sarai's opening solo in scene 3, "When I opened my tent". But these two themes, integrated in Sarai's opening solo, separate as the opera progresses, rejoined only in the epilogue in the solos and duets of Rebekah and Isaac. That is the only time when the love theme is used in a multi-voice piece; though there are earlier duets, trios and quartets, they are set to the friendship theme. Abram, significantly, never joins with another character in a duet. He is alone even at the beginning of the opera, when he loves Sarai, and becomes increasingly isolated as the opera progresses.

Above all, the music in <u>Sarai</u> is intended to strengthen and deepen the libretto's deeply affecting expression of Sarai's story, inviting you to share in her joy and her grief, her love and her despair.

# Cast of Characters

Eliezer, a man of Damascus and longtime servant of Abraham

Rebekah, the future wife of Isaac

Sarai/Sarah, Abram's wife

Abram/Abraham, patriarch of the family

Pharaoh, ruler of Egypt

Hagar, Sarai's maid and Abram's concubine, mother of Ishmael

Ishmael as boy, son of Abram and Hagar

Isaac as boy, son of Abraham and Sarai

Ishmael as adult

Isaac as adult

SARAI

# SARAI

## PROLOGUE

*The chamber opera starts out with a short prologue, which also
provides the framework for telling the story. Eliezer, who was asked by
Abraham to search for a wife for Isaac, and Rebekah, the chosen bride,
are traveling from Rebekah's childhood home near Haran to her new
place in Canaan, where she will stay at the side of her husband-to-be
Isaac. Eliezer, Rebekah and their entourage are about to end the day's
journey.*

*In the solo violin, we hear the echo of the shofar sound of hope, the
TEKIAH GEDOLAH.*

> *Rebekah:*
> We've traveled far, my friend.
> Let's rest and make a fire.
> And there with food and drink before us
> You'll tell me of the place I will call home.
>
> You've praised your master well
> Held in esteem the house of Abraham.
> Isaac's binding you related to my father
> And the pain this other father must have felt.
>
> Yet Isaac was son to a mother too,
> A woman teaching him of love and beauty.
> Who was she?
> And what do you know of her?
>
> *Eliezer:*
> She was indeed a splendid mistress,
> A princess with an ever open tent.
> Her dough increased tenfold,
> Her light burnt bright and steady

29

The entrance to her tent was crowned
By heavenly clouds.
Such was Sarai, your future husband's mother.
Throughout her life she loved and laughed and grieved,
A long and complicated story...

*Rebekah:*
Man of Damascus, you must tell me more!
For I'm to take her place in Isaac's heart.

*Eliezer:*
The story goes: When Sarai heard of Isaac's fate
She did emit six cries and wailings
Before her soul departed from her
And she perished. –
Alas, they got it wrong!

Although part of her soul has left her
When she heard of Abram's deed,
Sarai did not pass away.
Bravely she lived her life
Until her time on earth was up.
She did cry out though!
Six times
The shofar sounded.
And Isaac's mother
Voiced her joys and sorrows
To those willing to hear.

# SCENE ONE

*This scene is about the love of Sarai and Abram, their growing up together, their friendship, marriage, and life in Ur, then Haran. It ends with the call of God to leave the homeland and emigrate to "the land I will show you".*

*We hear the celebrating sound of the shofar, the TEKIAH, and then
Sarai's opening words corresponding to the TEKIAH.*

*Sarai:*
Praise be to God
For I knew the blessing of love.

When I opened my eyes
He stood before me,
Handsome, smiling,
With open face and open mind.

He guided me through childhood,
We laughed and played,
Shared chores and celebrations,
Year after year, until one day…

*Abram:*
…Looking at Sarai,
I was blinded by her beauty,
Her voice the only sound
I could still hear.
When she touched me
I changed from brother to lover
From childish boy to man.

You've moved my heart,
Sister and spouse.
With one gaze of your eyes
One link of your necklet.

*Sarai:*
I was yours, beloved,
And your desire was toward me.
You kissed my mouth
With kisses sweeter than wine.

31

*Abram:*
Many waters
Could not quench this love
Nor rivers flood it.
I was hers and she was mine.

*Sarai:*
As a fruit tree in the forest
So was my beloved among sons.

*Abram:*
As a rose among thorns
So was my beloved among daughters.

*Sarai:*
Abram then spoke these words
To take me with him
On life's journey:
"Arise, my fair one, come away.
Winter has passed,
The rain is o'er and gone.
The time of singing now has come
Let me hear your pleasant voice
Let me see your lovely face."

*Abram:*
And this was Sarai's wedding vow:
"Let us go out to the fields.
Let us see the vine flourish
And the tender grapes appear.
Where the pomegranate buds forth
I give you my love
And all the fruit I kept for you."

*Sarai:*
Our tent was strong as cedar
And our bed was soft and green.
Our love was strong as death,
Its fervor a great flame…

*Eliezer:*
Many a year they lived
In Ur as man and wife,
Took care of cattle and of sheep
And shared their joys and sorrows.

Thereon they moved to Haran
In search of fertile grounds,
And of the promised nation.
They hoped for sons
To carry on what they began.

Yet still, the couple was not meant to rest.
Abram again heard God's command
To break up camp,
And move to unknown lands.

# SCENE TWO

*Sarai and Abram traveling to Egypt. Abram asking his wife Sarai to act as his sister to protect his own life. Sarai in the harem at Pharaoh's court. Encounter with Pharaoh. Telling the truth about her marriage. Leaving with gifts and Hagar as a handmaid and friend.*

*We hear the wailing sound of the shofar, the SHEVARIM, and then Sarai's opening words corresponding to the SHEVARIM.*

*Sarai*
Have mercy on me, O God,
For I bore the betrayal of love.

As we moved on to distant lands
My husband too grew distant.
No longer could I see compassion
In his eyes, nor love nor laughter.
He spoke to God now, not his lowly wife.
His passion aimed for greater things
Than love between a barren couple.
The promises of God he lived for -
Whereas I put my faith in him, my man.

When we reached Egypt
On our flight from famine
Abram approached my tent
With this request:

*Abram:*
Sarai, you are a woman
Beautiful to behold.
When the Egyptians see us
As man and wife,
They will kill me,
And let you live
For your great beauty.
Say, you are my sister,
That it goes well with me
Because of you
And that my life be spared
On your account.

*Sarai:*
What could I say but: Yes,
I will do anything
To save your life, my love,
My brother and my spouse.

*Eliezer:*
When Egypt's princelings saw Sarai,
Bright as the morning star,
They praised her divine beauty.
Magnificent the prize they paid
To Abram for his sister:
Cattle and sheep,
Camels and asses,
Men and women slaves
Changed hands
Before Sarai herself
Was brought to Pharaoh's chambers.

*Instrumental interlude, retaking the sound of SHEVARIM, to mark the change of place within the scene.*

*Sarai:*
All through the night
I lay face down
And waited -
Waited to be raped.
Closed in by the dark
I pleaded with my God and with Abram.
But neither heard my cries.
Instead I heard the voice of Pharaoh
Wooing me with sweet words.

*Pharaoh:*
Behold, you are fair, beloved,
Behold you are fair.
Behind your veil
Your eyes are doves,
Your hair a flock of goats
Streaming down the slopes of Bakhu,
Your teeth white as shorn sheep
Who come up from their washing,
Perfect every one of them,

35

Your lips a scarlet riband
Gracing your lovely mouth.

Until the day breaks
And the shadows flee
I will hie to the mountain
Of myrrh and frankincense.
Come with me, my bride,
Come, my fair love.

*Rebekah:*
Sarai's new lord sounds kind and gentle,
He offered her his heart and land.
Did she still grieve for her lost love,
Long for her people, her own tent?

*Eliezer:*
Despair descended on her,
A gloom so deep it swallowed
Each and all in Pharaoh's house.
There was no joy in Egypt anymore.
Not one new child was born.
Life stood still.
At last Sarai told Pharaoh
The truth. She said:
"I am a married woman
And Abram is my spouse."

Pharaoh was well angry
With the man from Ur,
He scorned his guile.
For Sarai's sake though
He sent the pair away
Far richer than they came.

The mighty king commanded Hagar,
His own slave-daughter,
To serve the one
He himself would have loved to serve.

*Hagar:*
Sarai, my friend and mistress,
I am servant to my father's love now.
With Susinum I will anoint you
And dress you in a festive gown.
I will restore your star-like beauty
And see you home.

# SCENE THREE

*This scene focuses on the friendship of Sarai and Hagar, their living side by side in a male dominated world and giving each other comfort and joy and support. The scene ends with Sarai and Hagar agreeing that Hagar shall be surrogate mother for Sarai who cannot conceive a child of her own.*

*We hear the celebrating sound of the shofar, the TEKIAH, and then Sarai's opening words corresponding to the TEKIAH.*

*Sarai:*
Praise be to God
For I knew the gift of friendship.

When I opened my tent
She stood there, before me,
Beautiful, smiling,
With open face and open mind.

We saw ourselves as sisters
We laughed and cried,
Shared chores and celebrations,
Year after year, until one day…

*Hagar:*
...Looking at Sarai,
I could no longer bear
Her profound sadness,
The constant  yearning for a child.

Too strongly she reflected
My own need for a babe.
As handmaid far from home,
I was barren like her.

You move my heart,
Sister and friend.
In your eyes I see
The unborn son you grieve for each day.

*Sarai:*
And you, Hagar,
You look at children too
With longing and with love
And miss one of your own.

*Hagar:*
I am still young.
I could conceive
A child for both of us,
A baby with two mothers.

*Sarai:*
Are you in readiness
To take Abram as father of this fruit?
Will you lie with him
To come with child?
Do you feel strong enough
To face the pains of giving birth?"

*Hagar:*
I am prepared to do and bear
What any mother must endure.
To have a family.
And children of her own
For soul and spirit to live on
In future generations
For years and years to come.

*Sarai:*
As a fruit tree in the forest
So will be our son.

*Hagar:*
As a rose among thorns
So will be our daughter.

*Sarai and Hagar:*
Our child is coming,
Skipping over the mountains,
Jumping over the hills.
For winter has passed,
The rain is over and gone.
The time of singing has come,
Of singing a baby to sleep
With pleasant voices
In perfect harmony.

# SCENE FOUR

*The friendship of Sarai and Hagar is sorely tested when Hagar soon conceives a child by Abram. All relationships change. Sarai, Hagar and Abram have to find a new equilibrium. The life of the family and tribe is disrupted yet again when Abram enters his own covenant with God.*

## SARAI

*We hear the wailing sound of the shofar, the SHEVARIM, and then
Sarai's opening words corresponding to the SHEVARIM.*

> Sarai:
> Have mercy on me, O God,
> For I knew the falls of friendship.
>
> How are you, Hagar?
> Do you have good news for me?
>
> Hagar:
> Indeed, I do, my lady.
> What you failed to do
> For many years
> I did achieve
> In a short time:
> I am with child.
>
> Sarai:
> At last a time of singing!
> We'll sing a child to sleep:
> A fruit tree in the forest,
> A rose among thorns…
>
> Hagar:
> O, stop that childish talk, Sarai.
> Those were mere dreams.
> This is reality:
>
> I, the Pharaoh's daughter,
> Must no longer be
> A slave and stranger
> In your land.
> I am the mother now,
> Of Abram's son -
> And, I might add: I won his favor.

*Instrumental interlude, retaking the sound of SHEVARIM, to mark
the change of dialogue within the scene. Sarai now confronts Abram.*

> *Sarai:*
> May the wrong done to me
> Be upon you, my husband!
> I gave my maid to your embrace
> With pure intentions.
> Yet when she saw she had conceived
> She looked on me with great contempt
> And claimed she'd won your favor.
> Have you, again, betrayed our love?
> And sacrificed it for your visions?
> God shall be judge
> Of your life and of mine
>
> *Abram:*
> I singly did obey
> What God commanded:
> "Look toward heaven"
> He has told me,
> "And count the stars
> If you can number them.
> For so shall your descendants be."
> For this mission I forsake
> All mundane matters.
> The maid is yours,
> Do as you please.

*Instrumental interlude, retaking the sound of SHEVARIM, to mark
the change within the scene. Hagar tells of her flight into the desert and
her return to Sarai and Abram.*

> <u>Hagar:</u>
> When I carried Abram's child,
> Sarai treated me harshly
> And my lord neglected me.

I fled towards Egypt and
landed in the wilderness.

There by a spring
I met the grace of God
Whom I named Lahairoi,
The Living One That Sees Me.

The angel said he'd seen my sorrow.
He told me to go back
To fulfill my sacred duty.
My offspring would be greatly multiplied,
That was God's promise.
And so I bore a son
And named him Ishmael
For the God who hearkens.

*Sarai :*
Our child has come,
Skipping over the mountains,
Jumping over the hills.

*Hagar:*
For winter has passed,
The rain is over and gone.

*Hagar and Sarai:*
The time of singing has come,
Of singing a son to sleep
With pleasant voices
In perfect harmony.


*Instrumental interlude, retaking the sound of SHEVARIM, to mark
the last change within the scene. Eliezer tells us of the years after
Ishmael's birth and of Abram's covenant with God.*

*Rebekah:*
So Ishmael was raised
By both his mothers,
Two women who had dared
To be close friends again,
Sisters who had known
The falls of friendship?
Did they find new peace
Together as a family?

*Eliezer:*
They loved and tried,
Shared chores and celebrations,
Year after year, until one day…
… Abram, the aged patriarch,
Heard divine voices from above.
Who ordered him to change his name
To Abraham, father of many nations.
His wife, the mother of these peoples,
From now on should be called Sarah.

Abraham was full convinced
He read the word of God Almighty
Who offered him - and him alone -
An everlasting covenant:
The promised land of Canaan
Would be his forever,
The promised son by Sarah
Would finally arrive -
Provided that he cut
The flesh of his own foreskin
And of those living in his custody.

Obeying God's command.
Abraham took Ishmael,
His thirteen year old son,

And all the males
Who were born or bought
Into his house
And circumcised them
That very same day.

*Rebekah*:
Did not one single boy or man,
One mother, wife or sister,
Have any say in this?

*Eliezer*:
Our human dignity was sacrificed
For Abraham's grand mission.

# SCENE FIVE

*Announcement of Isaac's birth and Sarai's great joy in motherhood.
This scene contains the banishment of Hagar – seen as liberation to set
her free to build a life of her own, no longer slave to Abraham's house.*

*We hear the celebrating sound of the shofar, the TEKIAH, then Sarai's
opening words corresponding to the TEKIAH.*

*Sarai:*
Praise be to God
For I was given a son

I did laugh once, it is true,
At God's untimely promise.
Now only - an old woman -
I should have pleasure
With my lord
Him being old as well?

But then I chose
Hope against all hope,
Love over pride.
Back from Abimelech
And his unwanted favors
I did forgive my husband's
Disregard – again! -
For my well-being.

And at last my worn-out body
Conceived a child.
God has made me laugh
So all who hear this
Will rejoice with me
And my son will be named
Isaac, for he is laughter.

*Hagar:*
As a fruit tree in the forest
So will be your son.

*Ishmael (child):*
Your child has come,
Skipping over the mountains,
Jumping over the hills.

*Sarai:*
For winter has passed,
The rain is over and gone.

*Hagar, Ishmael, Sarai:*
The time of singing has come,
Of singing a baby to sleep
With all our voices
In perfect harmony.

SARAI

*Instrumental interlude, retaking the sound of TEKIAH but in its more urgent version, calling people together and pay attention to Isaac's circumcision*

*Sarai:*
The child was only eight days old
When Abram took him to his tent
And circumcised the little one
To please his mighty God.

The baby didn't cry long.
For I held Isaac to my breast
And stilled his pain.
His brother though, he wailed
All day and night
Until at last he fell asleep.


*Ishmael:*
I cry for baby Isaac
Feel sorry for his woe.
And for myself I cry as well
'cause I remember
What father Abraham
Has done to me
Not long ago
There in his tent.

I am afraid
Of things to come
In father's house.
What will befall my brother,
A tiny nursling
Who is already circumcised,
When he grows up
To be thirteen like me?

46

What other sacrifices
Are in store
For him, for me
And for our mothers
Just so the patriarch
Is able to fulfill
This secret sacred covenant?

*Instrumental interlude, retaking the sound of TEKIAH, in a calmer tone this time, calling Sarai and Hagar to discuss and plan their own future.*

*Sarai:*
I did give comfort
To my baby boy…

*Hagar:*
…and comfort was much needed
For his older brother.
We mothers helped each other out,
We saw ourselves as sisters.
We laughed and cried,
Shared chores and celebrations,
A few more years…

*Sarai:*
…yet we had made a plan
To shield our children
And ourselves
From further discreation
By Abram's zealous goals
For future generations.

*Hagar:*
Let him pursue his promised nations.
Meanwhile Sarai and I would tend
The land there is
And care for our people.

*Sarai:*
At the feast of Isaac's weaning,
Hagar and I decided,
I would give my handmaid and her son
The freedom she attempted once,
So many years ago, all by herself.

I would send the pair away,
With words as harsh as were before -
But this time with a few provisions
So they might find that well again
And put up camp,
My friend no longer slave
But her own mistress.

Isaac and I, we followed soon
Weaned from the bosom of Abraham
And met our sister and brother
In the wilderness that is Paran.

# SCENE SIX

*Scene 6 narrates Isaac's childhood with Sarai, Hagar and Ishmael; the boy's binding or sacrifice by his own father, and the return of Isaac and Ishmael back to Hebron and their mothers. Upon getting the news of Isaac's fate, Sarah cries out and faints. She and Hagar decide to part from Abraham and his religious dogma and to follow their own belief.*

*We hear the wailing sound of the shofar, the SHEVARIM, mixed with the alarming urgent sound of TERUAH, then Sarai's opening words corresponding to the SHEVARIM.*

*Sarai:*
Have mercy on me, O God,
For I was robbed of a son.

In the open lands of our exile
My loved ones stood beside me,
Steadfast, beautiful and smiling,
With open face and open mind.

We saw ourselves as family,
Two mothers and two sons,
Shared chores and celebrations,
Year after year, until one day…

My husband visited his sons
As was his right and custom.
This time though he requested
That Isaac join him on a journey.

*Abraham:*
I want to lead my son
From boy to man, bar mitzvah.
Together we will make our way
According to my God's command.

*Sarai:*
Abram, I'm weary of divine commands
You obey from high above.
Too well I know the toll
They take on human lives below.
Yet I am nothing but a woman.
You are the master of the house.
Go in peace, my husband.
Take young Isaac with you,
But take not him alone,
Let Ishmael, his brother, come with you
And Eliezer, our loyal servant, too.

*Instrumental interlude, retaking the sound of SHEVARI/TERUAH, to mark a change within the scene. Eliezer tells of the journey to the land of Moriah.*

> *Eliezer:*
> Three days we walked
> Towards the high land of Moriah.
> Then my master lifted up his eyes
> And far-off in the distance saw a cloud
> Resting on top of a mountain.
> He commanded Ishmael
> And me, his humble servant,
> To stay there with the ass.
> He and the lad went yonder,
> To worship their God.
> With a burnt offering.
>
> Abram put the wood on Isaac's back,
> Took the fire in his hand,
> Likewise the knife
> And they left together.
> Yet before the two did disappear
> Behind the mountain
> We heard them speak
> These words:
>
> *Isaac (child):*
> My father!
>
> *Abraham:*
> Here I am, my son.
>
> *Isaac:*
> Behold the fire and the wood,
> But where is the lamb for our offering?

*Abraham:*
God will himself provide a lamb.

*This instrumental interlude, retaking and expanding the sound of SHEVARIM, and TERUAH tells the most dramatic part of the Akedah, the Binding of Isaac, without words, using only sound and the imagination of the listeners to communicate the drama on Mount Moriah.*

*After a change within the scene, we are back at the camp of Sarai and Hagar, who are waiting for their sons' return.*

> *Sarai:*
> For weeks and weeks
> Hagar and I,
> Two mothers without sons,
> Shared chores and fears and worries
> Until one day…
>
> *Hagar:*
> Sarai, I see them coming!
> Back from the hills and mountains.
>
> *Sarai:*
> Winter has passed,
> The rain is over and gone.
>
> *Sarai and Hagar:*
> The time of singing has come,
> Of singing praise to our God
> With pleasant voices
> In perfect harmony.
>
> *Hagar:*
> How handsome is my Ishmael.
> And Isaac too,
> He's surely now become a man.

*Sarai:*
A greatly troubled man,
He has returned, our Isaac.
Where have you been, my son?
What was your fate?

*Isaac (child):*
My father took me up the mountains
And then down into valleys
And up a mountain yet again.
On top of it
He built an altar,
Arranged the wood,
Prepared the offering-place.
But there was no lamb.

Abba took the knife
To slaughter me instead.
I was afraid and helpless.
My hands and legs were bound.
I cried and wailed.
Then a great angel did appear.
He came from heaven
And called out to father:
"Lay not thine hand upon the lad,
And do not make a wound."

*Sarai:*
Woe unto you, my son!
Were it not for the angel,
You would have been slaughtered
There on the Mount?

*Isaac:*
Yes, mother.
Yes, I would have died.

*Sarai:*
No. No! No!!!
Woe. Woe! Woe!!!

*Sarai cries six cries corresponding to the three blasts of the shofar and three wails corresponding to the three ululations of the shofar. Then she faints, overtaken by her strong emotion.*

*Instrumental interlude, retaking the sound of SHEVARIM, in its most dramatic version, then calming down and fading away. Now we hear the TEKIAH GEDOLAH, a sound of hope, as Sarai is comforted by Hagar.*

*Hagar:*
Take heart, my sister,
For thankfully Isaac is saved
And safely back with us
As well is Ishmael.

*Sarai:*
I am aware of our good fortune,
And therefore try to make my peace
With Isaac's fate
And with my husband Abraham.

This man of God was lost
Without a sacrifice,
He needed well the emptiness of self
For his celestial communion.
You and I are different.
In every breath we draw
And then let out
We'll sense divine compassion.

We worship heaven
In the birth of our children,

In a moment of laughter
And in the hours of grief.

We see eternity
Not in the many sands
Along the edges of the seas,
But in a single grain of grit.

Each morning we say thanks
For getting back
Our blemished souls and selves
To celebrate another day.

*Ishmael (adult):*
Righteousness and justice
Are the foundation of God's throne.
Happy are we
Who walk in the light of great mercy.

*Isaac:*
We shall rejoice all day
And to praise divine favor
Take up the ram's horn
And make a jubilant sound.

*Hagar and Sarai:*
As fruit trees in the forest
So will be both our sons.
For winter has passed,
The rain is over and gone.

*Sarai, Hagar, Isaac , and Ishmael:*
The time of singing has come,
Of singing praise to our God
With pleasant voices
In perfect harmony.

# EPILOGUE

*Eliezer und Rebekah have traveled on. They meet Isaac, who leads Rebekah in his mother's tent. Isaac and Rebekah sing a love song that reminds us of Sarai and Abram and announces the beginnings of a new relationship and a new family.*

*In the solo violin, we hear the echo of the shofar sound of hope, the TEKIAH GEDOLAH.*

> *Eliezer:*
> My daughter, we are close now
> To your future husband's camp
> For he dwells here, in the South,
> Near the well of Lahairoi.
>
> *Rebekah:*
> Help me light off my camel,
> Eliezer, and tell me
> What man is this who walks
> There in the field to meet us?
>
> *Eliezer:*
> It is my master, Isaac.
>
> *Rebekah:*
> Quick, man of Damascus,
> Hand me my veil
> That I might guard
> My countenance.
>
> *Eliezer:*
> My master, we've come home
> From a long and arduous journey.
> I've brought your bride, Rebekah,
> Her beauty yet to be unveiled.

*Isaac (adult):*
Here, take some water, travelers.
Rebekah, still your thirst,
And wash your face,
Your hands, your feet.
Then I will lead you
Into my mother Sarai's tent
And take you as my wife.

 I will love you greatly
And myself be comforted
After my mother's death.
A dough again will rise,
A light burn bright and steady,
The entrance to our tent be crowned
By heavenly clouds.

You move my heart,
Sister and spouse,
With one gaze of your eyes,
One link of your necklet.

*Rebekah:*
I am yours, beloved,
And your desire is toward me.
You kiss my mouth
With kisses sweeter than wine.

*Isaac:*
Many waters
Will not quench this love
Nor rivers flood it.
I am yours and you are mine.

*Rebekah*:
As a fruit tree in the forest
So is my beloved among sons.

*Isaac*:
As a rose among thorns
So is my beloved among daughters.

*In this final aria, Rebekah and Isaac are accompanied by all the other characters. Everybody becomes part of the rich harmony.*

*Rebekah and Isaac*:
Our tent is strong as cedar
And our bed is soft and green.
Our love is strong as death,
Its fervor a great flame.

SARAI

# RUWTH

RUWTH

# Introduction

This chamber opera, the third in the series that began with <u>Yona</u> and continued with <u>Sarai</u>, is based on the <u>Book of Ruth</u> (phonetic transliteration: Ruwth). It is organized in five scenes and framed by a choral prologue and epilogue. Each scene is introduced and dominated by a different group of people (that is, a different chorus). All scenes except the last one end with a short interlude between Ruwth and her mother-in-law Na'omi.

The five scenes represent five different emotions or five philosophical concepts of relationships, not only between individual persons but also between communities and individuals:

> Scene 1: mistrust
>
> Scene 2: compassion
>
> Scene 3: loving-kindness
>
> Scene 4: justice
>
> Scene 5: reconciliation.

The story of <u>Ruwth</u> is not a dramatic fight between good and evil, but one of sharing and overcoming hardship. It shows that universal moral requirements sometimes must transcend or transgress particular communal standards. The two destitute widows Na'omi and Ruwth challenge the community to live up to its own ideals of inclusion. The outsider Ruwth overcomes the barriers of her home away from home with love, patience, and great courage.

Reflecting these themes, the music of <u>Ruwth</u> is less overtly dramatic than that of the two preceding operas, such as the storm music in <u>Yona</u> or the sacrifice music in <u>Sarai</u>. Instead, the central conflict between community and outsider, between native and foreigner, is expressed in the contrast between the string and harp orchestration for the characters of Ruwth and Na'omi versus the woodwind orchestration for the villagers. The contrast is also presented through the more jagged and discordant themes and harmonies that characterize the villagers early in Ruwth. The 3/4 meter of Ruwth's solos also contrasts both with the more irregular meters of the village women solos and with the restless 5/4 of Na'omi's early solos.

Mirroring the theme of community, choral settings play a more significant role throughout Ruwth than in the preceding operas. The final chorus, "While the earth endures", brings together Ruwth, Na'omi and Boaz with all the villagers. Each scene has at least one major chorus, though in Scene 1 the choral music is repeatedly interrupted by the gossip of the villagers.

The harmonic structure of Ruwth is different from that of the earlier operas, especially from that of Sarai. Unlike the conflict between the tonal centers of B-minor and F-minor in Sarai, the music in Ruwth progresses from an initial G-minor at the start of the opera to the related key of D-major by the end of the piece. Each of the four interludes is in the key of D-minor, the dominant to the G-minor key of the opera. The A-major tonality of the dance music at the start of Scene 3 helps to establish that piece as the center of the opera, midway in the transition from G minor to D-major.

While different from the first two operas, the music of Ruwth has many echoes of both Yona and Sarai. There are explicit quotes from both those earlier operas, most strikingly in the reprise of the "Benedicite" from Yona, set in 4/4 meter rather than 3/4 as in Yona. The 4/4 meter echoes the rhythm of the Israeli *hora*, with its characteristic long-short-short meter. The setting in Ruwth also reflects the more meditative mood of Scene Two, compared to the introduction of the "Benedicite" by the mariners in Yona. There are many other echoes of the music of

Yona and Sarai in Ruwth, such as in Scene Four's duet between Ruwth and Boaz that echoes Shachar's song at the center of Yona. Ruwth's opening solo in Scene One, reprised in Interlude Four, echoes the friendship motive of Sarai. The use of the harp as a frame for the interludes resembles the structural use of the shofar in Sarai. Similarly, the tambourine in Ruwth echoes the timpani of Yona.

These echoes and reflections of the earlier works help to establish Ruwth as the culmination and conclusion of the three operas. Both Shachar and Sarai are mentioned in the gossip at the start of Ruwth, bringing their stories back to mind. In the final choruses of Ruwth, the affirmation and peace that both Shachar and Sarai were able to find is re-affirmed for Ruwth, Na'omi, Boaz and all the members of the community in which they now participate. Like Shachar and Sarai at the end of their stories, Ruwth and Na'omi are not only supported by but participate in the enduring harmony celebrated in the music of Ruwth.

RUWTH

# Cast of Characters

Ruwth, a woman of Moab, daughter-in -law of Na'omi

Na'omi, a widow of Elim'elech,

Boaz, a landowner of Bethlehem

Boaz' Relative, a relative of Na'omi 's former husband

First village woman

Second village woman

Third village woman

Fourth village woman

Chorus of village women

Chorus of village men

First male harvester (overseer)

Second male harvester

Third male harvester

First and second female harvester

Chorus of male harvesters

Chorus of female harvesters

First village elder

Second village elder

Third village elder

Chorus of village elders

RUWTH

# RUWTH

## PRELUDE

*This opening chorus (adapted from Genesis 8:22, God's promise to Noah to never again destroy life on earth) has just one short verse, but as the words suggest, it should "never cease" – in the sense a Bach cantata seems to last forever and ever, thanks to fugue settings, variations etc. It is a joyful and rich song, sung by the full chorus, men and women together.*

*Between two renderings of the main poem, the women by themselves sing a second song. Its motive is Verse 5 of Psalm 126 - most famously set to music in Johannes Brahm's* German Requiem.

> *Chorus of village men and women:*
> While the earth endures,
> Summer and winter,
> Cold and heat,
> Day and night,
> Seedtime and harvest
> Will never cease.
>
> *Chorus of village women:*
> And may those who sow in tears,
> Reap with shouts of joy!
>
> *Chorus of village men and women:*
> While the earth endures,
> Summer and winter,
> Cold and heat,
> Day and night
> Seedtime and harvest
> Will never cease.

# SCENE ONE

*In the marketplace of Bethlehem, the village women are discussing
different things of interest. The price of the food, neighborly gossip.
This summer's harvest which promises to be so much better than in the
years before. The famine they experienced some years back. Somebody
remembers Elim'elech and Na'omi who had fled to Moab, the enemy's
land, during that time of dearth rather than to share their meager crop
with the starving neighbors of Bethlehem. The women wonder what has
become of the family. Somebody seems to have heard that Elim'elech
and also his two sons have died. Somebody else tells of the Moabite
wives that Na'omi's sons had married....*

*First village woman:*
Did you hear?
Sarai has
Born a son!

*Chorus of village women:*
Blessed be the Lord,
Who has not left her
Without next of kin.

*Second village woman:*
Did you hear?
The matchmaker went
To Shachar's house.

*Chorus of village women:*
Blessed be the Lord
Who brings her happiness
And children.

*Third village woman:*
Did you hear?
The price of grain
Is down today.

*Chorus of village women:*
Blessed be the Lord
Who gives us
Our daily bread.

*First village woman:*
I heard
The harvest will be good this year,
Barley and wheat are ample.

*Chorus of village women:*
Blessed be the Lord
Who came to us
After great hardship
To still our hunger
That we may live
And live abundantly.

*Fourth village woman:*
Speaking of hardship:
Did you hear
That Na'omi, who back then
With Elim'elech fled the famine,
Is on her way to Bethlehem?
She is a widow now
And without children.
Her husband and her sons have died
Away from home,
In the unclean land of Moab.

*Third village woman:*
I heard this was God's punishment
For leaving home and hearth
In times of great distress
Instead of sharing
Their rich crops with us neighbors.

*First village woman:*
That was so long ago!
Mahlon and Chilion
Were still children
In their swaddling clothes.
Do you think our Lord
Chastised even the babies
For their parent's fault?

*Second village woman:*
God did not doom the little ones,
But the grown men
Who took as wives
Orpah and Ruwth,
Daughters of our foemen.

*Third village woman:*
I heard,
The women of Moab
Are beautiful,
But dark of skin.

*Fourth village woman:*
And their ways are queer,
Outlandish and unseemly.

*Third village woman:*
Such foreigners do not belong
In our godly town of Bethlehem.

*Na'omi enters, followed by Ruwth. The women see them coming.*

*First village woman:*
Hear, hear!
Is this not Na'omi
Across the street?
Does she hear us? Na'omi!

*Na'omi:*
Do not call me Na'omi.
Do name me Mara,
Bitter of soul.
For the Almighty has dealt
Harshly with me.
I went away full
And he returned me empty.
Why call me Na'omi,
The beautiful and pleasant,
When the Lord afflicted me
And brought calamity upon me?
Woe is me!
For I am now
Without kin.

*Ruwth who is standing behind her mother-in-law turns to Na'omi and
tells her she is not alone*

*Ruwth:*
Did I, the older
Of your affinal daughters,
Not stay with you
And walk you to your people?
You are my only mother now
And I your family.

Entreat me not to leave you
Or keep from tending you.
For wherever you go,
I will go.
Wherever you stay,
I will stay.
Your people
Will be my people.
And your God
Will be my God.

Wherever you die
I will die,
And there I will be buried.
Nothing but death
Shall separate you from me.

*Na'omi and Ruwth embrace.*

*The chorus that follows is a more thoughtful version of the first chorus.
The women have heard what Na'omi and Ruwth had to say. They
learned of Ruwth's loyalty and make up their minds to offer them a
place to stay among them in Bethlehem.*

*Third village woman:*
Na'omi, we all heard
Your sorry tale of loss.

*Fourth Village woman:*
And we women fully know
The many hardships
Of a lonely widow's life.

*First village woman:*
We heard as well
The pledge and loving words
Of your adopted daughter.

*Chorus of village women:*
Blessed be the Lord,
Who has not left you
Without next of kin.

*Second village woman:*
There will be no place for you
At the inns of Bethlehem.
The landlords do not easily accept
Poor widows…

*Third Village Woman:*
...nor do they welcome
Strangers from Moab!

*First village woman:*
I heard there is an empty stable
Right at the edge of town.
It is a humble dwelling,
But dry and big enough for two.

*Second village woman:*
This shelter we can offer you
In the town of Bethlehem.

*Chorus of village women:*
Blessed be the Lord
Who grants mercy
To his prodigal daughters.


*Na'omi and Ruwth exeunt. The village women stay and discuss what happened.*


*First village woman:*
What a cheerless fate Na'omi suffered
In the foreign land of Moab.

*Second village woman:*
And to return without protection
But for a faithful - and foreign! - maid!

*Third village woman:*
How shall the two of them
Now make living
Among our people?

# INTERLUDE ONE

*In their new home, Na'omi and Ruwth make plans for their survival. Na'omi tells her daughter-in-law of her kinsman Boaz. Ruwth offers to go and glean in his fields.*

*Na'omi:*
What shall we do,
Both of us widows,
To make a life together
Here in Bethlehem?

I used to know,
Before I married,
A person of importance
Belonging to Elim'elech's kin.
But how can I now, a destitute,
Approach this man?

*Ruwth:*
Mother, please do not despair
Of our present  fate.
Let me go into the fields
And glean among the ears of grain.
The man in whose eyes
I might find favor
Will not berate me.

*Na'omi:*
Go, my daughter.
The Lord be with you.

# SCENE TWO

*In the fields, the harvesters sing working songs to make the time pass quicker and the hard work seem lighter. The song "O let the Earth Bless the Lord" is a quote from the first chamber opera of this trilogy <u>Yona</u>; it is part of the canticle "Benedicite" that is used in the Roman Catholic "Liturgy of the Hours" and also in Anglican and Lutheran worship.*

*The harvesters ask each other: "Did you see the maiden gleaning after the reapers?" Somebody heard it was the woman from Moab who came back to Bethlehem with Na'omi her mother in law. "Did you see how beautiful she is", one worker comments. Another says: "She working very hard." They tell each other how Ruwth has left her native country to be with Na'omi and support her. When Boaz comes, they tell him, that Ruwth had asked to glean his fields.*

*Chorus of harvesters:*
O you Mountains and Hills, bless the Lord
O all you Green Things upon the earth, bless the Lord
O you Fowls of the Earth, bless the Lord
O all you Beasts and Cattle bless the Lord
O you Children of Men, bless the Lord
Praise Him and magnify Him forever.

O Let Israel bless the Lord
Praise Him and magnify Him forever.

*First female harvester:*
Did you see the unknown maiden
Gleaning in our master's field?

*Second female harvester:*
Did you see how young
And beautiful she is?

*Second male harvester:*
We saw indeed her shapely form
Bending for some ears of barley.

*Third male harvester:*
We followed her
With our eyes
And with our lips we praised
Her sublime beauty…

*The female harvesters frown at this open admiration of the foreign woman.*

*First male harvester (overseer)*
…as we praise yours,
My lovely sisters,
As we praise female splendor
In each and every field.

*Enter Boaz.*

*Boaz:*
Reapers, did you see
The gleaning maiden in my field?
Who is that woman?

*First male harvester (overseer):*
She is a stranger,
A widow, who returned
With widowed Na'omi
From the land of Moab.

She came and asked
To glean and gather
Among the sheaves
When we are done.

According to the law
I gave consent.
She has since worked
Without a moment's rest.

*Enter Ruwth, still focused on her gleaning.*

*Boaz:*
May the Lord be with you, woman.

*Ruwth:*
And may He bless you, Master, and your crop.

*Boaz:*
Listen, my daughter,
Do no longer glean
In other fields.
Stay here and
Stay close to my maidens.
Let your eyes
Be upon the fields
Where they are reaping.

See, I have ordered
The men in my employment
Not to bother you.
When you are thirsty,
Don't hesitate.
Go to the water pots
And drink whatever
My servants have drawn.
When it is
Time to eat
Come over here
And have a meal.
You are most welcome
To eat our bread

And dip your morsel
In our wine.

*Ruwth bows deeply before the kindness of the man.*

*Ruwth:*
Why have I found
Favor in your eyes?
Why should you take notice
Of me, a foreigner?

*Boaz:*
I was told of all
That you have done for Na'omi.
How you left your parents
And your land of birth
For your chosen mother.
You came here to a people
You did not know before.
May the God of Israel
In whose presence
You take refuge
Bless you, my daughter,
And pay you full reward.

*Ruwth:*
You show great kindness,
My lord and master,
In speaking comfort
To the heart of your maidservant -
Though I am not even
One of your maidservants.

*The harvesters remind each other of Boaz' instructions not to molest the stranger, to let Ruwth glean with the maidservants, to even leave some extra sheaves for her and to offer her food and drink as long as the harvests of barley and wheat might last.*

*First female harvester:*
Did you see
How Boaz glared at our men
When they paid attention to the stranger?

*Second female harvester:*
Did you see
How he cautioned his young laborers
To leave the woman alone?

*First male harvester (overseer):*
Boaz commanded us
To let the woman glean
Even among the full stacks of grain.

*Second male harvester:*
Nobody shall reproach her.
We are to pull some barley from the bundles
As means for her to glean.

*Third male harvester:*
She's safe with Boaz and our maidens
Until all wheat and barley
Will be cleared.


*Chorus of harvesters:*
O you Heavens, bless the Lord
O you waters above the firmament, bless the Lord
O you Sun and Moon, bless the Lord
O you Stars of heaven, bless the Lord
O you Showers and Dew, bless the Lord
O you Winds of God, bless the Lord.

O let the Earth bless the Lord
For his mercy endureth forever.

# INTERLUDE TWO

*In their home Na'omi and Ruwth assess the situation, now that the harvests have come to an end. Na'omi tells Ruwth that she needs a home/husband (that would also secure the future of the mother-in-law). She thinks Ruwth should appeal very directly to Boaz their kinsman for protection, a man who already showed his loving-kindness towards Ruwth.*

*Na'omi:*
Should I not seek
A home for you?
Too soon the harvest season
Will come to an end.
You can no longer glean
In Boaz' fields.
Daughter, I must find
A place for you to settle,
A home,
Which will be good for you.

Why not woo
The one whose maidens
Were with you
For all these weeks?
Boaz is after all our kinsman.
I know, this very night
He will be winnowing
His barley at the threshing floor.
He spends the night there
To guard his grain.

Apace! Go wash yourself,
Put on perfume,
Don your best dress.
Then go down
To the threshing floor.

But wait until the man
Has finished eating
And drained his cup
Before you let him know
That you are there.

When he lies down,
Note the place.
As soon as he is resting,
Go over to him.
Uncover his feet
And lie down.
Have no fear,
My daughter.
He will tell you
What to do.

*Ruwth:*
Have trust in me,
My friend and mother,
All that you say I will do.

# SCENE THREE

*The singing and dancing men praise the rich harvest of this season. They praise God and toast their generous master Boaz who joins them in their song. A short while after, Boaz leaves the thanksgiving feast and goes to the threshing floor, where he has put up his bed for the night. Hie lies down and falls asleep. Ruwth comes in very softly and lies down at his feet. (The words of this harvest song are taken from Psalm 65)*

    *Chorus of Harvesters*
    Blessed be the Lord
    Who visits the earth,
    Gives it water

And makes it rich.
Your river, o God,
Is full of water
And you provide us
With a generous yield.

You drench our furrows
With great abundance
And soften the ridges
With gentle rain.
You bless all growth,
O Lord of the seasons,
And crown the year
With your bounty.

Wild grassland
Turns to pasture
And hillsides
Blossom with joy.
Meadows are clothed
With flocks of sheep,
Valleys are carpeted
With barley grain.

Let us shout and sing in exultation:
Blessed be the Lord!

*First harvester (overseer):*
Let us drink and salute
Our generous master!

*Chorus of male harvesters:*
To Boaz, the barley king!

*Chorus of harvesters:*
To Boaz! To Boaz!

*Chorus of harvesters:*
Blessed be the Lord
Who visits the earth,
Gives it water
And makes it rich.
Your river, o God,
Is full of water
And you provide us
With a generous yield.

Let us shout and sing in exultation:
Blessed be the Lord!

*Boaz exits the feasting scene and goes to the threshing floor. He lies down and falls asleep. Ruth enters and uncovers his feet. She lies down. At about midnight Boaz stirs and turns and finds the woman in his bed.*

*The threshing floor scene in this chamber opera is following closely the text of the King James Bible. Ruwth and Boaz narrate their encounter at night in direct dialogue. Boaz explains the details of the situation (closer kinsman) to Ruwth. Their duet is ending with the words: "Lie down until the morning".*

*Boaz:*
Who are you,
woman?

*Ruth:*
It is me, Ruwth,
Your maidservant.
Spread your skirt over me
And wed me
For you are next of kin,
And our redeemer.

*Boaz:*
Young woman,
This act of kindness
Exceeds all others.
You have not turned
To young men,
Rich or poor, for pleasure,
But sought
Redemption
For yourself
And your kinswoman.

Be not afraid,
Whatever you say,
I will do for you.
Everyone knows
You are
A marvelous woman.

*Short musical interlude, while Boaz thinks about the legal details of the situation.*

Now it is true.
That I'm a kinsman.
Yet there is a relative
Nearer than I.

*Ruwth is hiding her face, embarrassed by the awkward situation and very disappointed by Boaz' aloof behavior.*

*Ruwth:*
You do send me away then
From your harvest lodging?

*Boaz:*
No, no. Remain this night,
Young woman,

And in the morning
If the one closest
To the clan of Elim'elech
Will claim his right,
Let him do it.
If he's not willing,
I will act as next of kin
And release you
From your childless plight.

Lie down until the morning,
Ruwth. Please lie down.

*Ruwth:*
Boaz, I will lie down
Until the morning.
Spread your skirt over me
For you are my redeemer.

*Faintly in the background the by now tired harvesters still sing and praise their rich return.*

*Chorus of female harvesters:*
You drench our furrows
With great abundance
And soften the ridges
With gentle rain.
You bless all growth,
O Lord of the seasons,
And crown the year
With your bounty.

*Chorus of harvesters:*
Blessed be the Lord!

*The night wears away. The harvesters sing another verse or so, this time just humming, while the following short dialog takes place:*

> *Boaz:*
> The day is breaking, Ruwth,
> You have to go.
> No one shall know
> A woman came
> Down to my threshing floor.
> Take your shawl
> And hold it out
> So I can fill it,
> For you must not go empty-handed
> Back to your mother Na'omi.

# INTERLUDE THREE

*In their home Na'omi waits for Ruwth's return. She asks her how things went. Ruwth tells her of Boaz' generosity. Na'omi is hopeful regarding their future.*

> *Na'omi:*
> How are you, my daughter?
> How did you fare?

> *Ruwth:*
> I did remain the night
> For Boaz spread his skirt o'er me.
> He promised me
> To act as our redeemer.
> He said I must not return
> Empty-handed.

> *Na'omi:*
> Then all is well.
> Stay here, my daughter,

And await what comes to pass.
For this man will not rest
Until the matter is resolved
And he made you as his spouse.

*Na'omi looks out window and sees Boaz.*

I see that Boaz gathered the elders
Already at the city gate.


# SCENE FOUR

*At the city gate Boaz has gathered the relative of whom he had spoken.*
*He also called on ten of the elders to fill the quorum for witnessing*
*Boaz' transaction with the next of kin. The elders discuss the business*
*at hand and they attest that you can only claim the land of a deceased*
*relative if you also give protection to the widow and perpetuate the*
*name of the family. They agree that only Boaz is ready to fulfill the law*
*in its entirety.*

*Instead of by a chorus, as in scenes one to three, this scene begins with*
*an instrumental prelude that sets the scene. We now sit among the*
*gossiping elders of Bethlehem.*

*First village elder:*
Did you know
The barley harvest
Was plentiful this year?

*Second village elder:*
And the wheat
was copious too.
Blessed be the Lord!

*Third village elder:*
Did you know
That our Boaz
Let a woman from Moab
Glean in all his fields?

*First village elder:*
That goes against tradition!
Our gleaning laws should
Benefit our own people!

*Second village elder:*
But widowed Na'omi
*Is* one of us.
And her daughter Ruwth
Has gleaned for her...

*Third village elder:*
...and has worked hard
All through the harvest season.
I heard that Boaz has acted toward her
With exceeding kindness.

*First village elder:*
Do you think
He will redeem her
And make her
His wife?

*Second village elder:*
I think there is another man
Closer still to Elim'elech
And his family.
He might lay claim
To his rights
And acquire land and woman.

*Third village elder:*
I know for sure
That Boaz wants
To settle the question
This very day.

He asked us all
To come and
Offer counsel
In this matter.

*First village elder:*
What do you know!
Here Boaz and the kinsman
Both come to the gate.

*Boaz and the relative arrive and sit down with the elders. Boaz begins to speak.*

*Boaz:*
Widow Na'omi has returned from Moab
And is about to sell her husband's land.
You, kinsman, have first right
And I come after you.
In the presence
Of the elders of my people
I ask you:
Will you redeem it?

*Relative:*
Without a doubt:
I will redeem.

*Boaz:*
The day you buy the field
From the hand of Na'omi

You also accept Ruwth,
Woman of Moab,
Widow of Na'omi's late son.
This is in order to restore the name
Of the dead upon his inheritance.

*Relative:*
Count me out then!
I want the land, but not the woman.
I have a wife already
And might destroy
My own inheritance
By raising children of another clan.
I am not willing to redeem.
The right is yours.

*The relative leaves in great haste. Boaz addresses the Village Elders.*

*Boaz:*
I will redeem land and family.
Here is my sandal to confirm.

*The following somewhat prosaic words of Boaz in front of the elders are also in a way his love song and his official proposal to Ruwth.*

*Boaz:*
Ruwth is to be my wife!
Blessed be the Lord.

Elders, you bear witness
That I have bought from Na'omi
All that belonged to Elim'elech
And to his sons.

I take title too
To the spouse of Mahlon

So his name will not be cut
From the place he came from.

You are witnesses this day
That I gained Ruwth,
Woman from Moab,
And spread my skirt over her.

Ruwth is to be my wife!
Blessed be the Lord.

*Chorus of village elders:*
We witnessed your vow.
May God make the woman
Who enters your house,
Fruitful as Sarai, Rachel and Leah
Who built the house of Israel.
May you do well
And gain fame in Bethlehem.
And may you prosper
Through the children
God will give you
By that young woman.

*Boaz exit. The Elders repeat their benediction.*

We witnessed his vow.
May God make the woman
Who enters his house,
Fruitful as Sarai, Rachel and Leah
Who built the house of Israel.
May he do well
And gain fame in Bethlehem.
And may he prosper
Through his children.

# INTERLUDE FOUR

*In their home Na'omi and Ruwth discuss the newest development.
Ruwth assures Na'omi of their ongoing commitment to each other.*

*Na'omi:*
Call me Na'omi again,
For I am redeemed.
The name of Elim'elech will live on.
And you, my daughter,
Will at last have a home,
A husband and soon children.


*Ruwth*:
You are still my mother though,
And I your family.
My marriage makes me not leave you
Or keep from tending you.
For wherever I go,
You shall go.
Wherever I stay,
You shall stay.
Your people
Are now my people.
And your God
Has become my God.
Whenever I give birth
You will give birth,
And my children will be yours.
Nothing in life
Shall separate you from me.

*Ruwth and Naomi:*

For wherever I go,
You shall go.
Wherever I stay,
You shall stay.
Nothing in life
Shall separate you from me.


# SCENE FIVE

*The village women celebrate the birth of Ruwth's son as a restoration
also of Na'omi's life. They praise Ruwth' loving-kindness, and call her
the one "who is more to you (Na'omi) than seven sons". And they
name the boy Obed: the one who serves.*

> *First village woman:*
> A son has been born
> To you, Na'omi,
> The beautiful and pleasant.
> He will give you new life
> And take care of you
> In your old age.
>
> *Chorus of village women:*
> Blessed be the Lord
> Who has not left you
> Without next of kin.
> May his name
> Be celebrated
> In all of Israel!

*Second village woman:*
Your daughter Ruwth,
Who loves you,
Is more to you
Than seven sons.
She has born
You a child.

*Chorus of village women:*
We give him the name of Oved.
Since he is the one
Who serves and fulfills
The blessings of the Lord.

*The village men join the women in a recapitulation of the prelude-song, which has two elements: the everlasting promise (never ceases) and the promise of hope (may those who sow in tears).*

*Chorus of village people, with Ruwth, Na'omi and Boaz:*
May those who sow in tears,
Reap with shouts of joy!

*Chorus of village men and women:*
While the earth endures,
Seedtime and harvest,
Day and night
Cold and heat,
Summer and winter,
Will never cease.

www.ingramcontent.com/pod-product-compliance
Lightning Source LLC
Chambersburg PA
CBHW071619040426
42452CB00009B/1404